And The Rain Falls

Jorge Henri

BookLeaf Publishing

Presentation by *BookLeaf Publishing*

Web: www.bookleafpub.com

E-mail: info@bookleafpub.com

ISBN: 9789357444804

First edition 2023

For my light and my love. You have brought me back from the edge and shown me the sun. I love you Skittles.

ACKNOWLEDGEMENT

For all of those who touched my life. This book belongs to you all.

PREFACE

These poems were written from a place of loss. During these dark times while suffering from the loss of several loved ones I truly found the brightest lights in my life.

And The Rain Falls

Grey,
The world loses it's color,
Staccato tapping against the pane,
Sadness creeps in,
A mourning of the light,
Water covers all,
In a lonely room I sit,
And the rain falls,
I feel tired,
I feel old,
Looking out a window,
Distant from the world,
And the rain falls,
Missing your touch,
Having you here,
My heart breaks,
Mourning your loss,
And the rain falls,
The world turns,
Passing day to day,
I sit in a lonely room,
And the rain falls.

Dark Happy Days

My dark happy days are gone,
Replaced by blinding light,
Judged by others and told I was wrong,
Assured that they were right,
I changed my life to fit,
Filed my rough edges down,
Changed everything and here I sit,
Alone without a sound,
They called me strange,
They called me weird,
Thought I was deranged,
Into the crowd I was steered,
Now into this magicless world I live,
Still alone in this crowd,
No one here to blend in with,
And I couldn't be less proud,
I miss the night,
I miss when I was free,
I wish I could back out of the light,
I wish I were me.

You

A miracle was given to me,
Graced pure and true,
My heart is full for all to see,
All because of you,
Your eyes so bright,
and filled with care,
Fills my life with light,
And my heart beams from your stare,
You are beautiful and giving,
To everyone regardless of merit,
Happiness is what you bring,
And I don't want to share it,
Your touch electric,
Your smile brighter than the sun,
You make my heartbeat hectic,
You make my life fun,
Your love is my world,
I'm happy when you are near,
You make my head whirl,
And fill me with cheer,
Together we are entwined,
Together we two,
My life is better inclined,
All because of you,
So when I hear,

Footsteps at my door,
I always hope it's my dear,
The one that I adore.

Words

A thousand vines,
Coming from all around,
With their stoning spines,
Dragging me down,
Pulling me under,
As I gasp for air,
Filling me with wonder,
Drowning in despair,
I can see a light,
Much too far to reach,
With every breath I fight,
Fighting to breach,
I see people on shore,
Shouting and trying to help,
Screaming words but no more,
I scream and I yelp,
Their words flaccid,
Against the vines they have no effect,
My lungs burn like acid,
I fight to stay erect,
I catch words in the air,
Everyone trying to aid,
Trying to care,
But my will starts to fade,
Waiting for someone,

To do something for me,
They all seem done,
And leave me be,
I fought and I struggled,
All through this hell,
A war that had you bugged,
Locked in this shell,
The fight raged on,
A pain I could not bear,
Waiting for a new light to dawn,
To awaken from this nightmare,
Pulled downwards,
I look to the sky,
You offered only words,
Even now as I die.

Winter

Icy frost,
Deep blue lake,
Mountainous beauty,
Dangerous for all,
Her fingers twist,
And tangle in our hair,
Freezing our noses,
Crystallizing our eyes,
She starts so gentle,
But her touch you still feel,
As her grip tightens,
And locks you in place,
Animals die,
Trapped by the cold,
Her heart freezes,
All but the hardiest of blood,
The beauty of snow clouds,
And drifts to the sky,
Winter birds chirping,
The bluest of blue skies,
Just when you think it will all stay,
It all begins to melt,
And the temperatures climb,
You long for her touch,
As flowers and trees start to bloom,

But she'll return quick,
She'll come again just as you forget,
Of her hard embrace,
She's dangerous to love,
But beautiful to see,
She'll make you wish for warmth,
And though you stand by the fire,
She'll leave you cold inside,
And freezing within.

Hope

Cherry blossoms bloom,
Green grasses and leaves growing,
Hope and spring returning.

Four

We both have legs,
But you have four,
Yet some say,
That I'm worth more,
You love whole heart,
And I love with conditions,
My love is quite tart,
While yours is unrestricted,
You love regardless of creed,
I pick and choose,
You love without need,
I love for desire,
Even if mistreated,
Or beaten,
After a long day I'm still greeted,
Still loved and kissed,
Even when things worsen,
You gaze longingly at me,
As if I were the best person,
You make me question all logic,
And the definition of love,
As you adore us all,
With a heart from above,
You fill my heart,
Wether lazy,

Or mischievous,
You're as cute as a daisy,
And just as marvelous,
So still I ask why I'm valued more,
Just because I have two legs,
And you have four.

Longing

I still look for you,
Though you no longer see,
I listen for you too,
But you can't hear me,
My heart longs for you,
Your's can't feel at all,
Where you are I have no clue,
Sometimes I feel you here,
And yet not to be found,
I like to think you're near,
But you're not around,
It burns my soul,
That I can't tell you how I feel,
I'm getting old,
And losing my will,
I long to be where you are,
If I could only find a way,
No matter if I travelled by plane or car,
Not night or day,
Can I reach where you exist,
I can only hope,
That I make that list,
Still I walk and still I lope,
Til the end of my days,
After my travels are done,

May we entwine out ways,
And may together they always run.

Water

Blue, wet, cool,
Touching and engulfing,
Hot yet cold,
Natures lifesblood,
Blue, wet, warm,
We bask and play,
Engulfed in your embrace,
We bring you everywhere,
Blue, wet, hot,
We use you to wash, cook, bathe,
And keep us warm,
Blue, wet, cold,
Your mysteries confound us all,
All of the life you support,
All of the life you heal,
There is not enough thanks,
We could not live without you.

Anxiety

I feel you choking me,
Cutting off my air,
Chest is full of fire,
As I long for control,
Everyone around is unaware,
As I fight for my life,
Right in front of them,
They laugh,
They joke,
They ask how I am,
But they don't care,
I am drowning,
Swallowed by the immenseness,
And all I want is to be normal,
But all I feel is overwhelmed,
I feel alone,
Isolated,
I can't hide,
I can't run,
Stop,
Please just stop,
But it never does,
It keeps pace,
It escalates,
Then de-escalates,

It hides within,
Waiting til I am unaware,
Waiting for the perfect surprise attack,
I just want my normal back.

My shadow

The smell of the air,
Green grass between my toes,
A day without a care,
Wind tickles my nose,
The sun high and bright,
Making my shadow big,
Try as I might,
I can’t lose it if I zag or zig,
It follows me everywhere,
Doing as it will,
I’ve seen it here and there,
Hardly stands still,
No matter what I wear,
I’ve seen it scared,
I’ve seen it brave,
Clothed or bared,
Even when I shave,
I like its shape,
Though it could slim down,
I’d like it better with a cape,
Or shaped like a clown,
My shadow has never left my side,
Never came to my aid,
Watching from the outside,
Never seems to fade.

Night's Knight

When Night's knight comes calling,
On a Cool Autmn eve,
The sound of his hooves are made of hellfire,
They shine with an umber glow,
Flames licking the ground with each step,
His armor is Black as the void,
The pull you feel when he draws near,
It seeks out the lonely, the desperate, the unfair,
His sword glows like the light of the full moon,
But offers no comfort,
The light within shimmers with frost,
You can feel it tug at your soul,
And will end you in a powerful thrust,
The souls of those already taken,
Scream when he holds it on high,
Trying to claw out of the prison,
That they built themselves,
His gaze cold as the frost on the ground,
He searches for outsiders,
Walking alone,
He takes them all,
For evil or for good,
Adding to his might,
Strong willed,
And tenacious in his hunt,

Once he has your scent,
He never gives up,
He stalks dark and empty places,
And Joyous places too,
Coming for those lost souls,
Who happen to be blue,
So if the autumn moon rides high in the sky,
And you find yourself out of sorts,
Find shelter quickly,
Or we may find you no more.

My creator

Your light touches us all,
Creator of great and small,
Grateful of you we are,
Even when we feel subpar,
As children can be,
We don't seem to hear,
And we cannot begin to see,
How your miracles appear,
You shape our earth,
Everyday it changes,
From the light of every hearth,
All of the rearranges,
You make us better,
Than we ever thought we'd be,
You know us to a letter,
Every I, U, and Tee,
Every night I pray,
To better understand,
I worry the things I say,
Might not make me the best human,
But lord I love you,
And will do as you assign,
I know others love you too,
And have faith in your design.

Present

These devices we hold in our hands,
That hold us captive every day,
Blind us from seeing what is real,
And in front of our eyes,
These thieves are stealing from you,
Precious moments you'll never get back,
Some people are waiting to hear your voice,
And you keep putting them off,
Some people might be near,
Others may be far away,
Some might be across the room,
Wondering where you are,
These moments you are missing,
Can never be returned,
All the life points that are left,
Unnoticed,
Unloved,
Untouched,
Before you search for the next relic,
Before you up your level,
Maybe you should show up for real,
And be the hero others know you to be,
Not in these fake worlds,
But in this one,
A moment of your kindness,

Could save someone,
Could help someone,
A moment where you were there,
To listen,
To share a smile,
A moment to be present,
In this present that was given,
To all of us,
To share,
Whether good or bad,
Just to tell us about your day,
And share,
These things,
Steal your life a second at a time,
All of your posts,
Your tweets,
Your videos,
Are they worth your life?
Are they worth your time?
Scrolling endlessly,
Through a sea of monotony,
Missing the things,
You'll never see again.

Inside

There's a monster in me,
Not sure how he came to be,
He attacks at will,
Lashing out and won't be still,
It hurts the ones I love,
From those below to above,
It can never be done,
It rips people to shreds for fun,
It knows how to wound,
And can always be found,
Claws sharp as knives,
Teeth ready to bite into lives,
Eyes always looking for easy prey,
The ones that are just in the way,
The ones that offended and call,
And the ones that did nothing at all,
I am not sure how it came to be,
But beware! There's a monster in me.

You

You are special,
You are loved,
You make my heart flutter,
And burst at your smile,
You light up my life,
Like the sun at midday,
You make my face hurt,
Smiling ear to ear,
When you are asleep,
I can't wait to hear your voice,
Telling me your dreams,
Your hopes,
And your fantasies,
You make me feel,
Make me understand,
Make me believe,
That there is still good in this world,
Your smell lingers,
In every room,
When your gone,
I long for your touch,
I wait with baited breath,
For your return,
I long to hold you in my embrace,
Feel your arms around me,

It doesn't matter,
If it was days or hours,
Feeling you next to me,
Is all that matters.

Missing You Missing Me

I've been missing you,
you've been away,
every minute,
Of every day,
you left me here,
on my own,
it was clear,
we were done,

But I'm still missing you,
Missing me,
broke my heart,
And you were free,
a little note,
And one goodbye,
All your kisses,
All your lies,
It took a while now to see,
That I'm missing you missing me,

Your picture hangs,
Up on the wall,
Damn it stings,
That you won't call,
Tell me girl,

what have I done,
you were my pearl,

But I'm still missing you,
Missing me,
broke my heart,
And you were free,
a little note,
And one goodbye,
All your kisses,
All your lies,
It took a while now to see,
That I'm missing you missing me,

Then last night,
In the bar,
felt just right,
Just like it should,
saw your ring,
your left hand,
Just another thing,
You hurt me again,

But I'm still missing you,
Missing me,
broke my heart,
And you were free,
a little note,
And one goodbye,

All your kisses,
All your lies,
It took a while now to see,
That I'm missing you missing me.

Soda

Frosty cool taste,
Bubbles fizzing up my nose,
Refreshing to feel.

Momo

Blacker than night,
Eyes of yellow,
You are quite the sight,
And an awesome fellow,
You jump and leap,
And knock things over,
Sometimes you peep,
And hide in the clover,
Your white spots are awesome,
Your ears expressive,
Your leaps better than some,
But I think they're impressive,
Your purrs are quite loud,
Your claws are fine,
I am very proud,
That you are mine.

The Play

The snap happens,
And everything starts,
A blur of motion,
As the quarterback drops back,
The receivers racing their routes,
With extreme balance and grace,
One of the defenders grabs one,
By the mask on their face,
The quarterback scans the field,
Facing left when he sees,
His receiver running down the seam,
He's running fast,
But the coverage is tight,
He lets the ball go,
In a practiced balanced release,
The ball spirals through the air,
A work of art in motion,
As the ball begins it's descent,
The reciver jukes,
Making distance,
He looks up and reaches out,
And the ball drops perfectly,
Into his hands,
He pulls the ball in with care,
As he breaks the plane,

The crowd roars,
And comes to life,
The team joins in as well,
One single play,
Lasting seconds for most,
But lingers for a lifetime,
In a memory.

Cooking

Fire heat seasoning,
Flames cooking food with good care,
A deft form of art.

www.ingramcontent.com/pod-product-compliance
Lightning Source LLC
Chambersburg PA
CBHW051747130826
49812CB00033B/1035
* 9 7 8 9 3 5 7 4 4 4 8 0 4 *